WITHDRAWN

DOWNSIDE
OF DRUGS

ADHD Medication
Abuse

Ritalin®, Adderall®,
& Other Addictive Stimulants

DOWNSIDE of DRUGS

ADHD Medication Abuse: Ritalin®, Adderall®, & Other Addictive Stimulants

Alcohol & Tobacco

Caffeine: Energy Drinks, Coffee, Soda, & Pills

Dangerous Depressants & Sedatives

Doping: Human Growth Hormone, Steroids, & Other Performance-Enhancing Drugs

Hard Drugs: Cocaine, LSD, PCP, & Heroin

Marijuana: Legal & Developmental Consequences

Methamphetamine & Other Amphetamines

New Drugs: Bath Salts, Spice, Salvia, & Designer Drugs

Over-the-Counter Medications

Prescription Painkillers: OxyContin®, Percocet®, Vicodin®, & Other Addictive Analgesics

DOWNSIDE OF DRUGS

ADHD Medication Abuse

Ritalin®, Adderall®, & Other Addictive Stimulants

Rosa Waters

Mason Crest

Mason Crest
450 Parkway Drive, Suite D
Broomall, PA 19008
www.masoncrest.com

Printed and bound in the United States of America.

First printing
9 8 7 6 5 4 3 2 1

Series ISBN: 978-1-4222-3015-2
Hardcover ISBN: 978-1-4222-3016-9
Paperback ISBN: 978-1-4222-3189-0
ebook ISBN: 978-1-4222-8802-3

Cataloging-in-Publication Data on file with the Library of Congress.

Contents

INTRODUCTION

One of the best parts of getting older is the opportunity to make your own choices. As your parents give you more space and you spend more time with friends than family, you are called upon to make more decisions for yourself. Many important decisions that present themselves in the teen years may change your life. The people with whom you are friendly, how much effort you put into school and other activities, and what kinds of experiences you choose for yourself all affect the person you will become as you emerge from being a child into becoming a young adult.

One of the most important decisions you will make is whether or not you use substances like alcohol, marijuana, crystal meth, and cocaine. Even using prescription medicines incorrectly or relying on caffeine to get through your daily life can shape your life today and your future tomorrow. These decisions can impact all the other decisions you make. If you decide to say yes to drug abuse, the impact on your life is usually not a good one!

One suggestion I make to many of my patients is this: think about how you will respond to an offer to use drugs before it happens. In the heat of the moment, particularly if you're feeling some peer pressure, it can be hard to think clearly—so be prepared ahead of time. Thinking about why you don't want to use drugs and how you'll respond if you are asked to use them can make it easier to make a healthy decision when the time comes. Just like practicing a sport makes it easier to play in a big game, having thought about why drugs aren't a good fit for you and exactly what you might say to avoid them can give you the "practice" you need to do what's best for you. It can make a tough situation simpler once it arises.

In addition, talk about drugs with your parents or a trusted adult. This will both give you support and help you clarify your thinking. The decision is still yours to make, but adults can be a good resource. Take advantage of the information and help they can offer you.

Sometimes, young people fall into abusing drugs without really thinking about it ahead of time. It can sometimes be hard to recognize when you're making a decision that might hurt you. You might be with a friend or acquaintance in a situation that feels comfortable. There may be things in your life that are hard, and it could seem like using drugs might make them easier. It's also natural to be curious about new experiences. However, by not making a decision ahead of time, you may be actually making a decision without realizing it, one that will limit your choices in the future.

When someone offers you drugs, there is no flashing sign that says, "Hey, think about what you're doing!" Making a good decision may be harder because the "fun" part happens immediately while the downside—the damage to your brain and the rest of your body—may not be obvious right away. One of the biggest downsides of drugs is that they have long-term effects on your life. They could reduce your educational, career, and relationship opportunities. Drug use often leaves users with more problems than when they started.

Whenever you make a decision, it's important to know all the facts. When it comes to drugs, you'll need answers to questions like these: How do different drugs work? Is there any "safe" way to use drugs? How will drugs hurt my body and my brain? If I don't notice any bad effects right away, does that mean these drugs are safe? Are these drugs addictive? What are the legal consequences of using drugs? This book discusses these questions and helps give you the facts to make good decisions.

Reading this book is a great way to start, but if you still have questions, keep looking for the answers. There is a lot of information on the Internet, but not all of it is reliable. At the back of this book, you'll find a list of more books and good websites for finding out more about this drug. A good website is teens.drugabuse.gov, a site compiled for teens by the National Institute on Drug Abuse (NIDA). This is a reputable federal government agency that researches substance use and how to prevent it. This website does a good job looking at a lot of data and consolidating it into easy-to-understand messages.

What if you are worried you already have a problem with drugs? If that's the case, the best thing to do is talk to your doctor or another trusted adult to help figure out what to do next. They can help you find a place to get treatment.

Drugs have a downside—but as a young adult, you have the power to make decisions for yourself about what's best for you. Use your power wisely!

—*Joshua Borus, MD*

1. WHAT ARE ADHD MEDICATIONS?

ADHD medications are drugs that are meant to treat attention-deficit/hyperactivity disorder. There are several different kinds of medicines that can help people with ADHD. These include Ritalin®, Adderall®, Dexedrine®, Vyvanse®, as well as others. They're usually pills, although there's one kind that's a skin patch. Most of them belong to a type of drugs that are called stimulants.

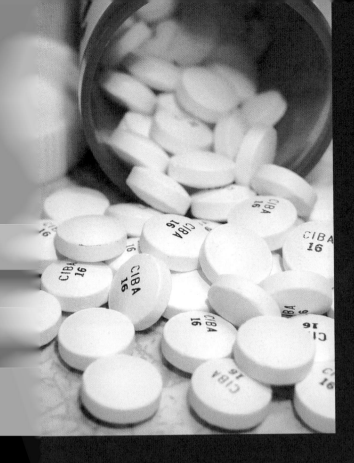

Sometimes kids who have a *prescription* from their doctors for this medicine abuse the pills. They take more of them than they're supposed to take. And kids who don't have ADHD sometimes abuse these medicines too. They like the way the pills make them feel.

When young people abuse ADHD medications, they often crush the pills and snort them up their noses. This gets the chemicals in the pills into their blood faster than if they swallowed them. It speeds up the pills' effects on their brains and the rest of their bodies.

ADHD medications can help people who have ADHD. But these drugs also have a downside.

ADHD
Attention deficit hyperactivity disorder

Attention deficit hyperactivity disorder (ADHD), similar to hyperkinetic disorder in the ICD-10) is a psychiatric disorder of the neurodevelopmental type in which are significant problems of attention and are not appropriate for a person's twelve and be present for m school-aged individual

Despite b

2. WHAT ARE THE DOWNSIDES OF THESE DRUGS?

When these drugs aren't taken for ADHD according to a doctor's instructions, they can be dangerous. Some of them are addictive, and all of them have *side effects*. They can make people feel good—but they can also make people feel pretty bad.

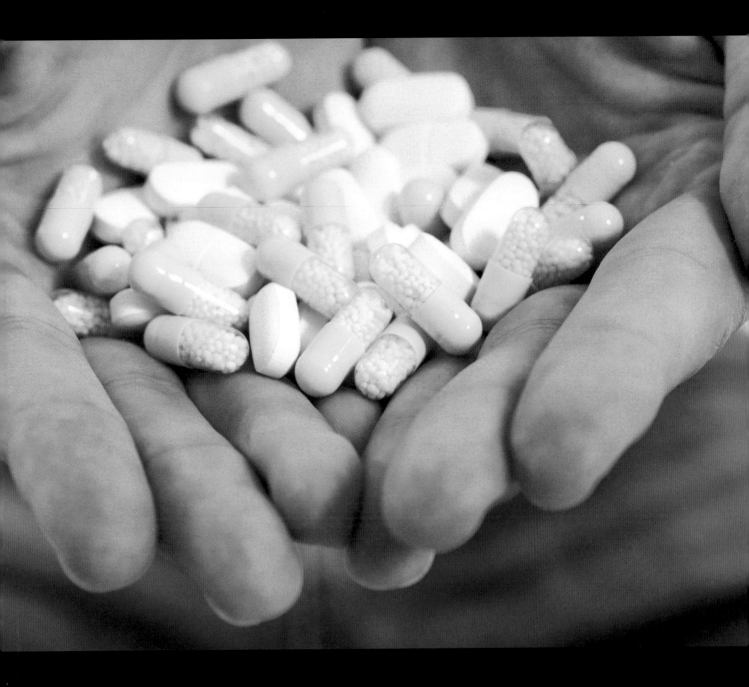

If you take an overdose of these medications, you could seriously hurt yourself. You might even die. That's a pretty big downside!

Most ADHD medications are stimulants. This means that they're the kind of drug that speeds up your body's actions. They make your brain work faster. If you're taking a stimulant, you'll feel more alert and wide awake. You may feel as though you have more energy. You'll probably be in an "up" mood too. You could feel happy . . . or you could feel REALLY, REALLY happy.

These drugs also make you breathe faster. They make your heart beat faster. They make the blood push harder and faster through your veins.

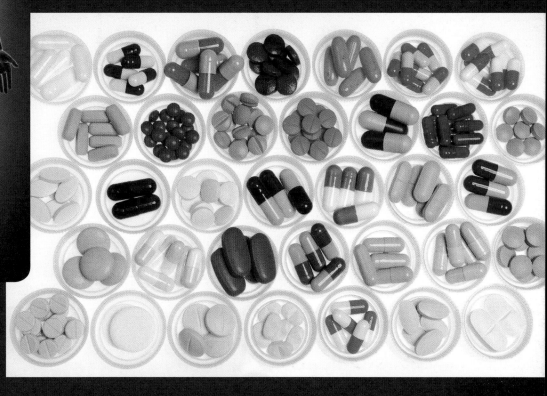

There are many kinds of stimulants. Some of them are legal. Caffeine is a legal stimulant that's found in coffee and many soft drinks. Cough medicines sometimes have stimulants in them. Doctors use other stimulants to treat *depression*, as well as ADHD. Some stimulants only affect certain organs in the body, so doctors might use one of these stimulants to treat someone whose heart has stopped. The right kind of stimulant could get the heart beating again.

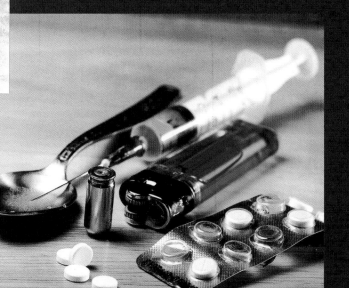

Others stimulants are illegal. Cocaine, amphetamines, and meth are all illegal stimulants. These drugs don't come from doctors. Instead, they're made illegally, and they're sold on the street. But legal or illegal, almost all stimulants can be abused. And when they're abused, they're dangerous.

4. WHAT IS ADHD—AND WHY ARE THESE DRUGS USED TO TREAT IT?

ADHD is a medical condition that starts when you're a kid. If you have ADHD, it may be hard for you to sit still and pay attention in school. You may be fidgety and do things on impulse. This could get you in a lot of trouble at school! Of course all of us act like this once in a while, but people who have ADHD have brains that work a little differently from other people's. People with ADHD can't always help the way they behave.

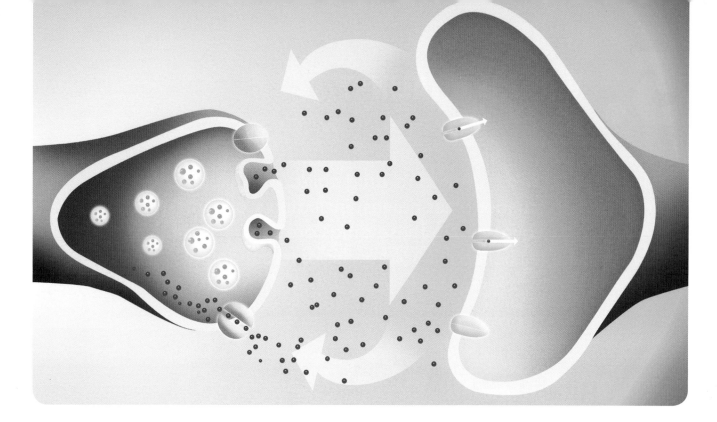

Doctors aren't sure what causes ADHD, but they do know that it is has something to do with changes in brain chemicals called neurotransmitters. Brain cells are very, very small, of course, but if you could see what was going on inside your brain between the cells, it would look something like this picture. There are tiny gaps between each cell. The neurotransmitters (shown above as little dots) are the chemicals that help carry messages across those tiny gaps. Different neurotransmitters help the brain do different jobs. The neurotransmitter dopamine, for example, is what gets the brain's attention center working. People with ADHD may not have enough of this chemical inside their brains.

This is where ADHD medications can help. The brain is made of nerve cells, which are long, spidery-looking cells. The messages that flow between them are like electrical currents—and the neurotransmitters are the connectors that allow the current to flow. Some kinds of ADHD medicines keep the neurotransmitters from being absorbed back into the cells. Other kinds of ADHD medicines help the brain cells make more of these chemicals. Either way, the brain has more dopamine and other neurotransmitters to pass along the messages that help the brain to focus.

5. WHAT IS RITALIN®?

Ritalin is the **brand name** for a drug called methylpenidate. The same drug is also sold under other names, including Concerta, Methylin, Daytrana, and Equasym XL. These drugs are all the same thing as Ritalin. The same chemical is sold under different names.

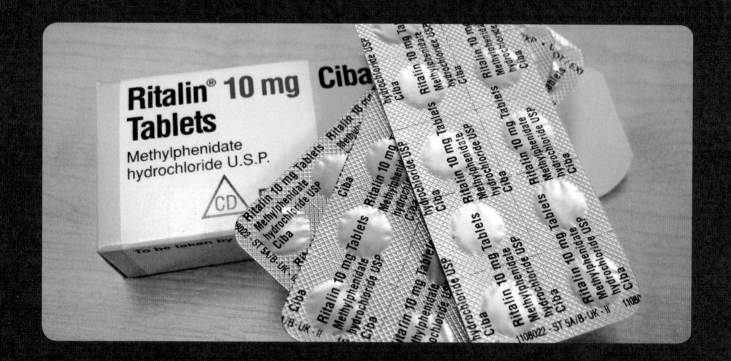

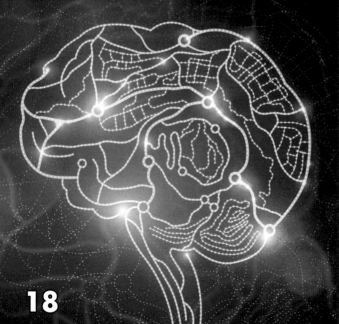

Methylpenidate increases dopamine in the brain. It also raises the levels of another neurotransmitter, called norepinephrine. It keeps these brain chemicals from being absorbed back into the brain's cells, which means there are more of them to carry messages between nerve cells.

When taken at the correct dose, the chemical in Ritalin helps people with ADHD think more clearly. It helps them to focus on tasks better.

Ritalin and the other drugs that contain methylpenidate can also have side effects. The most common are nervousness, sleepiness, or *insomnia*. Other side effects are also possible. When these drugs are abused, they can be far more dangerous.

Ritalin has lots of street names. Some of these are Rids, Vitamin R, Kibbles and Bits, Kiddy Cocaine, Skittles, and Smarties.

6. **WHAT IS ADDERALL®?**

Adderall's chemical makeup is different from Ritalin's. It is an *amphetamine*. It works by triggering the brain to release more dopamine and norepinephrine, the neurotransmitters that help memory, learning, focus, and problem-solving. These neurotransmitters also create pleasure and good moods, which is why people sometimes abuse these drugs. When not used correctly by people who have ADHD, Adderall is far more dangerous than Ritalin.

Students who do not have ADHD sometimes take Adderall to help them study and do better on tests. Other young adults abuse Adderall *recreationally*. The pills can be ground up and snorted up the nose or *injected* into the blood. Sometimes, people who abuse Adderall also do something called "stuffing" — they stick a wad of the ground-up pills into their nose, mouth, vagina, or anus, which makes the drug's effect last a long time.

Adderall has lots of side effects. Most of these are usually mild when someone who has ADHD takes the drug at the correct dosage. When it is taken at higher doses, though, it can cause serious physical and *psychological* problems, including addiction.

Adderall has several street names, including: Speed, Beans, Black Beauties, Christmas Trees, and Double Trouble.

7. WHAT ARE SOME OF THE OTHER STIMULANTS USED TO TREAT ADHD?

Dexedrine is another stimulant drug that's used to treat ADHD. It is made from the chemical dextroamphetamine. It's also sold under the brand names ProCentra and Dexstrostat. Like Adderall, it is a very dangerous drug when abused.

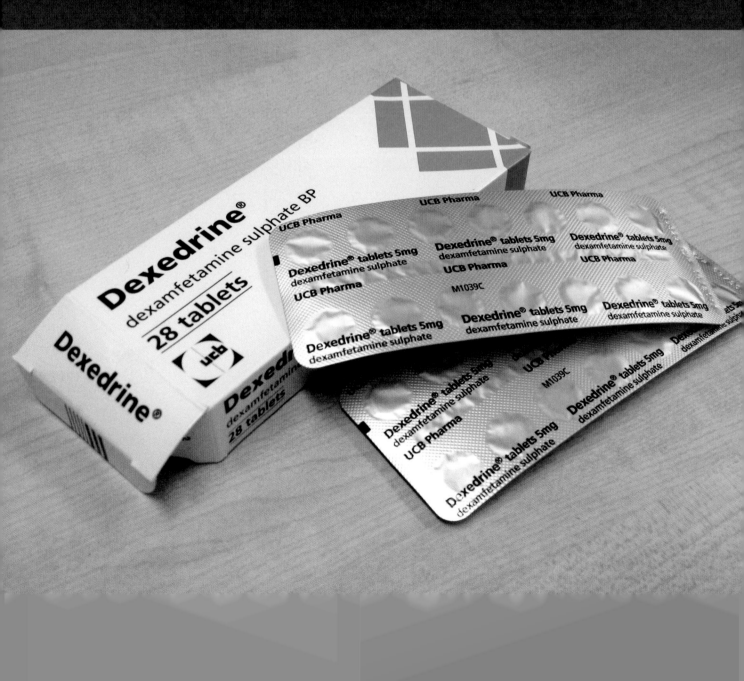

Dexedrine can cause many unwanted symptoms. A few of these are insomnia, stomachaches, tiredness, and nervousness. It can also have more serious side effects, especially when it's been used for long periods of time. When Dexedrine is abused, it can cause addiction. It can have seriously bad effects on a person's body and mind, including heart problems and *hallucinations*.

Some of Dexedrine's street names are Bennies, Hearts, and Dexy's Midnight Runners.

8. WHAT IS THE HISTORY OF ADHD MEDICATIONS?

1880s

The first amphetamines were made. Back then, doctors didn't know how dangerous many of these drugs would turn out to be.

1

2 Doctors began to notice that students with learning problems did better when they took some of these stimulant medications, and the U.S. government approved Dexedrine as a medicine for kids with attention problems.

1930s

1957

Ritalin in made for the first time. At first, it was used to treat people who had problems with tiredness and sleepiness.

3

4 Doctors began to use Ritalin to treat ADHD. Adderall was made about the same time.

1960s

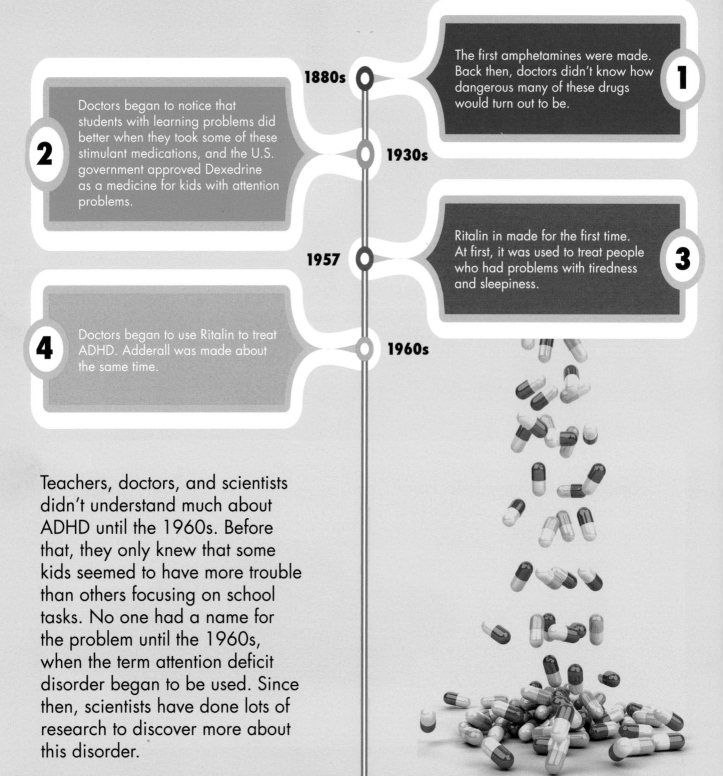

Teachers, doctors, and scientists didn't understand much about ADHD until the 1960s. Before that, they only knew that some kids seemed to have more trouble than others focusing on school tasks. No one had a name for the problem until the 1960s, when the term attention deficit disorder began to be used. Since then, scientists have done lots of research to discover more about this disorder.

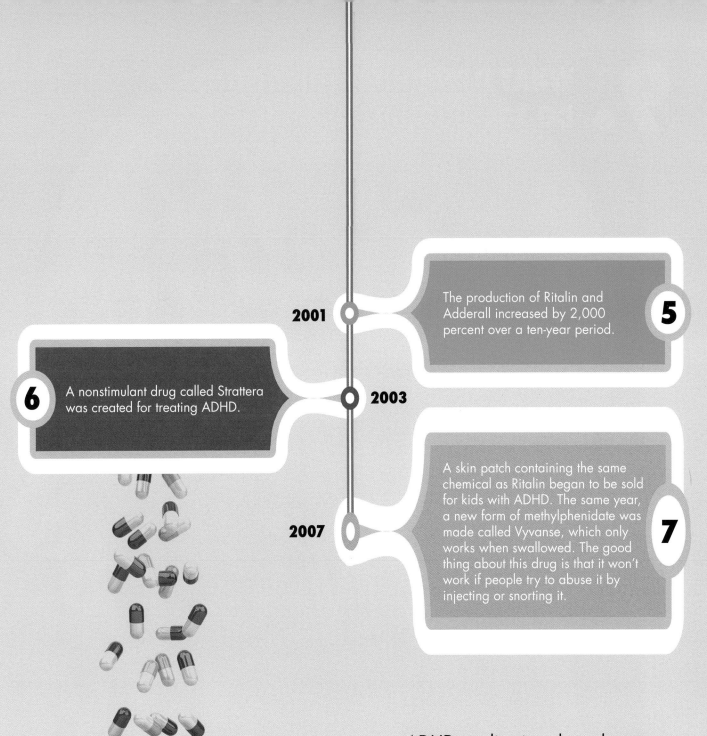

2001

The production of Ritalin and Adderall increased by 2,000 percent over a ten-year period.

5

6

A nonstimulant drug called Strattera was created for treating ADHD.

2003

2007

A skin patch containing the same chemical as Ritalin began to be sold for kids with ADHD. The same year, a new form of methylphenidate was made called Vyvanse, which only works when swallowed. The good thing about this drug is that it won't work if people try to abuse it by injecting or snorting it.

7

ADHD medications have become more and more common over the years. The U.S. Drug Enforcement Agency says that there are 500 percent more prescriptions being written for these drugs to-day than there were in 1991. With so much of these drugs out there, it's become easier and easier for people to get them and use them recreationally.

WHAT DO ADHD MEDICATIONS DO TO YOUR BRAIN?

When someone takes a stimulant drug regularly, the brain can come to depend on the chemicals in that drug. If she tries to stop taking it, she will feel *anxious*, grumpy, and tired. She may feel so sad that she wants to kill herself.

This is what happens when someone is addicted to a drug. It's one of the most serious things that ADHD medications can do to your brain.

Another possible side effect of ADHD medications is seizures. A seizure happens when the messages between the brain's cells get overloaded. It's as though all the nerves sent messages all at the same time. This can make the person twitch and shake. He could lose consciousness.

Abusing these drugs can also make your brain play tricks on you. They might make you feel as though people are out to get you. (This is called paranoia.) You might feel angry all the time, even though there's nothing really to feel angry about. The drugs could make you see things that aren't there (hallucinations) or believe things that aren't true (delusions). You might feel very confused.

10. WHAT DO ADHD MEDICATIONS DO TO YOUR BODY?

Abusing ADHD medications can damage your body as well as your brain. These drugs can keep your body's systems from working the way they're meant to work. They can make your heart beat too fast. You might have a hard time breathing. They could make your nose and mouth very dry.

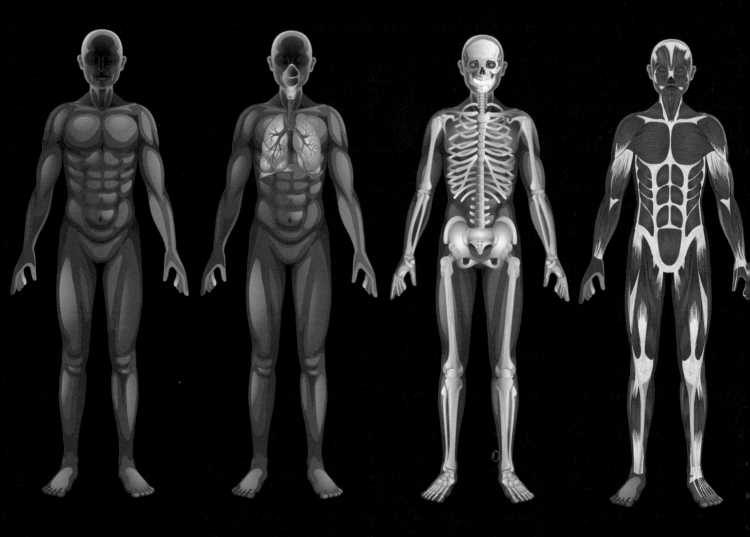

Taking too much of these drugs too often could make your blood pressure go so high that you could have a stroke. (A stroke is what happens when a blood vessel in your brain bursts. If the brain is damaged, you might not be able to speak or move normally—or it could kill you.)

Abusing these drugs often could also cause weight loss. This might seem like a good thing if you think you have a few pounds you need to lose—but the drugs can get in the way of your body getting the nutrition it needs. That's a big problem for a teenager, whose brain and body are developing so quickly. You might stop growing normally.

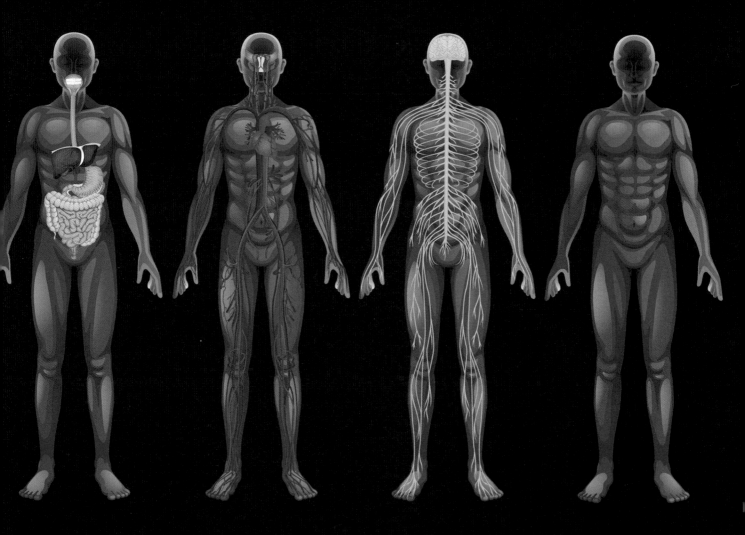

11. WHY ARE ADHD MEDICATIONS ADDICTIVE?

When someone has been taking these drugs regularly over a period of time, the brain may come to depend on them. It will no longer be able to produce the neurotransmitters the nerve cells need to manage emotions.

This will mean that the person can't feel happy in the normal way. The everyday things that give us pleasure—like friends and games and good food, for example—will no longer interest her. Instead, she will need to take more and more of the drug in order to feel happy. She may need the drug just to get through the day. Without it, she will be too tired and sad to do much of anything.

12. WHY DO TEENAGERS ABUSE ADHD MEDICATIONS?

Some teenagers who don't have ADHD take Adderall, Ritalin, and other ADHD medications because they think these drugs will help them do better in school. High school students (and college students too) take the drugs so they can study harder and longer, and so that they can concentrate while they're taking tests. They may even think these drugs will make them smarter.

A study done in 2012 by the U.S. National Institute on Drug Abuse found that 10 percent of high school sophomores and 12 percent of seniors admitted to using a "study drug" that was not prescribed by a doctor. In high-achieving high schools, as many as 40 percent of the students are taking these drugs, hoping that the medications will help them get better grades.

Other teenagers take these drugs to get high. They like the excited, happy feeling the drugs give them.

Teenagers often think that ADHD medications are safe because they're legal. They don't realize that these drugs are powerful chemicals that can hurt their bodies and minds. And they won't make them any smarter than they are already!

According to the study done by the Institute on Drug Abuse, about 2.7 million adolescents have abused either Ritalin or Adderall at least once in their lifetime, while 1.9 million have abused one of these drugs in the past year.

In the past eight years, calls to poison-control centers about teens who have abused ADHD drugs have increased by 76 percent.

13. HOW CAN YOU TELL IF SOMEONE IS ABUSING ADHD MEDICATIONS?

Here are some signs of stimulant abuse:

- problems in school
- change in activities or friends
- long periods of sleeplessness or not eating
- memory lapses
- unusual behaviors, including unexplained spending
- mood swings and being unusually grouchy
- weight loss
- *dilated* pupils, dry mouth and nose

HOW CAN YOU TELL IF SOMEONE YOU KNOW IS BECOMING ADDICTED TO ADHD DRUGS?

- The person may prefer to be alone more than before.
- The person can no longer function in school or at work.
- The person starts to get in trouble at school or with the law.
- Relationships with friends and family break down.
- The person may no longer shower or change clothes as often.
- The person has money problems, because he is spending so much money getting drugs.
- The person is willing to go to any effort to get her drugs.

14. IS IT A CRIME TO ABUSE ADHD MEDICATIONS?

Even though these drugs are legal, you're only supposed to take them if a doctor says you need them. Without a doctor's prescription, the sale, possession, and use of drugs like Adderall is a *felony*. If you're caught, you could end up paying a heavy fine or spending some time in jail.

If you get caught abusing ADHD medications, you could also end up with a record that could hurt your future. Getting arrested doesn't look good to colleges, and it won't impress your future employers!

15. WHAT HAPPENS IF YOU MIX ALCOHOL AND ADHD MEDICATIONS?

It's a really bad idea to mix alcohol with any drugs. Even if you take ADHD medications because a doctor has said you need them and you never take more pills than you're supposed to, you still need to be very careful about alcohol.

The chemicals in ADHD medications can make it hard for you to feel the effects of alcohol. This could mean that you keep drinking because your body isn't sending you any warning signals that you're drunk. But even though you don't *feel* drunk, your body will still respond to the alcohol. You could suddenly pass out. You might vomit. You could get alcohol poisoning and have to go to the emergency room.

A few years ago, a college freshman was drinking whiskey and taking Adderall to have a good time. He was a perfectly healthy young man—but he ended up in the hospital with a heart attack.

What should I do if I think someone has overdosed on ADHD medications?

An overdose is when someone takes too much of any drug or medication, so that it causes serious, harmful symptoms or even death. If you think you or someone else has overdosed on a drug, you should always call 911 immediately. If it's not an emergency but you have questions about preventing an overdose, you can also call the National Poison Control Center (1-800-222-1222) from anywhere in the United States. It is a free call and it's *confidential*. You can call for any reason, 24/7.

My doctor has prescribed ADHD medications for me—but if they are so dangerous, should I take them?

If you have ADHD, these medications can help you out a lot. You shouldn't be afraid to take them, so long as you totally follow your doctor's instructions. But keep a few things in mind:

- Don't ever think that if one pill helps you, two will be even better! Only take the amount your doctor says you should.
- Never, ever share your medications with friends.

If you don't take the medicines you need to help your brain, you'll have more problems at school. These medications can also help you handle social situations better. And researchers have found that kids with ADHD who *don't* take these medications are more at risk for abusing other more dangerous drugs. ADHD medications have a downside—but they also have an upside!

FURTHER READING

Bestor, Sheri Mabry. *Substance Abuse: The Ultimate Teen Guide.* Lanham, Md.: Scarecrow Press, 2013.

Edelfield, Bruce. *Drug Abuse.* New York: Rosen, 2011.

Herzenak, Joe. *Why Don't They Just Quit?* Loveland, Colo.: Changing Lives Foundation, 2010.

Magill, Elizabeth. *Drug Information for Teens: Health Tips About the Physical and Mental Effects of Substance Abuse.* Detroit, Mich.: Omnigraphics, 2011.

Nadeau, Kathleen G. *Learning to Slow Down & Pay Attention: A Book for Kids About ADHD.* Washington, D.C.: Magination Press, 2004.

Nelson, David. *Teen Drug Abuse (Opposing Viewpoints).* Farmington Hills, Mich.: Greenhaven Press, 2010.

Parker, Charles. *The New ADHD Medication Rules: Brain Science & Common Sense.* New York: Koehler Books, 2012.

FIND OUT MORE ON THE INTERNET

ADHD

kidshealth.org/teen/diseases_conditions/learning/adhd.html

ADHD and Stimulant Medication Abuse

www.add.org/?ADHDstimulantabuse

DrugFacts: Stimulant ADHD Medications

www.drugabuse.gov/publications/drugfacts/stimulant-adhd-medications-methylphenidate-amphetamines

How Stimulants Affect the Brain and Behavior

www.ncbi.nlm.nih.gov/books/NBK64328

Misuse and Abuse of ADHD Medication

www.clinicaladvisor.com/misuse-and-abuse-of-adhd-medication/article/189985

GLOSSARY

amphetamine: A synthetic, addictive drug used to treat ADHD. It is also used illegally as a stimulant.

anxious: Nervous or worried.

brand names: Names given to a drug by the company selling them. Usually, the name is easier to say and remember than the longer chemical name.

confidential: Kept secret.

depression: A feeling of powerful hopelessness and sadness, which usually lasts for a long time.

dilated: Expanded.

felony: A major crime. Being convicted of a felony usually results in a prison sentence.

hallucinations: Things you see and hear that aren't really there.

injected: Used a needle to put a drug straight into the bloodstream.

insomnia: A condition where you are unable to sleep.

prescription: A note given by a doctor with instructions to take a certain drug. You can only legally buy certain drugs if you have a prescription saying that you need to take that drug.

psychological: Having to do with the mind or the study of the mind.

recreationally: Done for fun. When talking about drugs, it's when you use a drug to get high instead of to treat pain or an illness.

side effects: Effects that a drug might have other than the intended effect. Usually, side effects are unpleasant.

INDEX

PICTURE CREDITS

ABOUT THE AUTHOR AND THE CONSULTANT

ROSA WATERS lives in New York State. She has worked as a writer for several years, producing works on health, history, and other topics.

DR. JOSHUA BORUS, MD, MPH, graduated from the Harvard Medical School and the Harvard School of Public Health. He completed a residency in pediatrics and then served as chief resident at Floating Hospital for Children at Tufts Medical Center before completing a fellowship in Adolescent Medicine at Boston Children's Hospital. He is currently an attending physician in the Division of Adolescent and Young Adult Medicine at Boston Children's Hospital and an instructor of pediatrics at Harvard Medical School.